BIG TOWN BLUES

DYLAN HARRIS

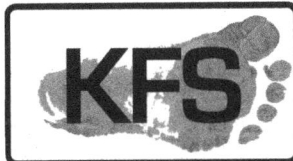

KFS

NEWTON-LE-WILLOWS

Published in the United Kingdom in 2018
by The Knives Forks And Spoons Press,
51 Pipit Avenue,
Newton-le-Willows,
Merseyside,
WA12 9RG.

ISBN 978-1-912211-18-0

Acknowledgements:

versions of some poems are published in: *the liberation of [placeholder], the smoke, Blue & Yellow Dog, ditch, E ratio, nth position, Sun sh, upstart.ie & Upstairs at Duroc.*

Supported using public funding by
ARTS COUNCIL ENGLAND
LOTTERY FUNDED

BIG TOWN BLUES

CONTENTS

since the day is wasted

since the day is wasted
it might as well be wasted
writing in a pub

writing

i'm not even kidding myself

degraded stress

my psyche
   is degrade
      to surface

my converse
   is degrade
      to silence

less coffee
   no class
less tech
   no stress

apparently a vacation
   reduces intelligence
      by 10%

hey—
i'm on half a dozen holidays

heh—
i'd better set a project

denk zul

sky up
the looking

song then singer

everyday
pock *kühl*

eye then brow

walk bow
dank lid

beer then nausea

pub sweet
into

open the chaos

up the kriek

there are
in the reports of the great
beer critics

super brews
noted the best in the world
rightly

and the ordinary
sold like cuttle
ordinary

and in the poetry
clattering around like undercarriage
there are names

the ordinary
why does prose use the special
poetry the ordinary

kirin my arse
i'm invading the verbiage empire
stealing geuze

seeking blonde
in the boot of my lies
& gorgonzola

for the smell
that was supposed to be golden charles
my foot

it's not the ads
their Fear and Loathing
their Fortified Fluff

it's the intensity
yes the sensual intensity
the flavour's the dance

hey poets here's a €7 note
of course it's a €7 note
it says so

where i wrote it

the conversatiee

i approach the cut
  as though i make
    machinery

the detail revolution
  each day
    the whole is boiled

the conversatiee
  looks to the route he expects
    the whole is lava

i let my art
  give me the sleigh

if it's not on his plot
  it doesn't exist

he'll know more
  i'll be more

pupate

there is the sphere
there
there is the wrinkle
there

the surface
the wrinkle
your life
there

it's the wrong wrinkle
it's old like the scoundrels next door
it's the wrong wrinkle
pupate

pupate
the planet
the sphere's a sac
pupate

blue and green and gas
the sphere
there

pupate

veer horizon

colouring the converse air
a massive sewn masterpiece
tapestry of night
you can't take the thought away

not the moon setting
the sun

through dark form
released rising
the city burns

the foreground
a house a park
whole
one window
lit by sodium
that's all

the dark detail between
you perceive trees
wild old wood
edge of the eye movement

tension
disaster grasps
the wood awaits the flame

but are you reading this
into the picture's black
or inventing

it's the frame
old master wood reused
formally decorated
and burning
the corners are burning

burning from the fire in the city
burning from the memories
yours
you're the one burning the sewn
you're the one burning the frame

look away
don't let your history flaunt
it burns

but you want that
don't you

the sea

on my wall
you'll see
the sea

it's just the waves
the grey waves
the sky

there's no ship
it's just the sea
the ship's sunk
it's just the sea
there's no ship
it's just the sea
the waves

on my grandmother's wall
you'd have seen
the sea

there's no ship
it's just the sea
the waves
the grey waves
it's just the sea

her youngest brother
died in the last ship
the last torpedo
a hundred year ago

her favourite brother
the last torpedo
a century

it's just the sea
there's no ship
the sea
the ship's sunk
it's just the sea

on my wall's
a picture
the sea
it's just the sea
the grey waves
the grey sky
the sea

it's just the sea
the ship's sunk
it's just the sea
the grey waves
the sea

her brother

the sea

it's just the sea

her brother

the ship's sunk

it's just the sea

the sea

the sea

My grandmother's youngest brother died on the last British ship sunk in the great war.

it's process

you do understand
it's process
the poem is process

between the dug
& the out
is the digging

process

the vibrate

the phone's in the pocket
it's on vibrate
it doesn't bloody vibrate
but you take it out
check

the suspicious tickle
the vibrate that isn't ...

what does it say
i don't like what's said
you know what is says
i don't like what's said

the vibrate
the fictious vibrate

the alone

cross tension

chorus
cross tension
across the light
    the light
cross tension
across the light
    the light

the anti–energy's
anti–glow

chorus

the anti–energy's
anti–glow

the man
who presses
whose pressing pulls
    it pulls

chorus

the anti–energy's
anti–glow

the man

who presses

whose pressing pulls

    it pulls

doesn't see

doesn't look

    just pushes

doesn't see

doesn't look

    just believes

chorus

the anti–energy's

anti–glow

the man

who presses

whose pressing pulls

    it pulls

doesn't see

doesn't look

    just pushes

doesn't see

doesn't look

    just believes

we tell him
we tell him
    he barracks
we barrack
we barrack
    he weeps

chorus

at the delicious life

do you wonder
when you look
across that chasm

at the delicious life
the playful to accompany
the wrapping the double

do you not wonder
might it be better
to be
where the chasm's
a stream

in the marsh
at the sucking graves
of the armies
of lone action

the graves
the child me
was learned

i built this city
here
myself
it was the only place

it's falling down now
the damp degrades fine structure
like stars stretch

a rope and a rocket
i wonder

would the sky be tied
would i trust the tied
could i cross
would i return

being the smog

i like climbing up
i love the up tops
i adore the glorious air

but when i'm up top
it's always too low
there's another higher i know

chorus

i look at the map
the very drunk map
it focuses only the now

the coming down's bad
the valley's much worse
the smog the terrible smog

i follow the map
my very own map
avoiding the dangers of tales

chorus

people tied to their graces
lost in their places
smart me for walking beyond

i keep going to where
the map says it's there
the map says the ocean's a tree

chorus

but i've already climbed three
a revelationary three
their cool and glorious air

i've time for two more
mur de temps

leek & stilton

i'm in a pub
that doesn't serve food
remembering a pub that does

both places i've written
for whatever it's worth
they play the musical naff

it's in the write

i hope you buggers
in the future
have found a cure
for the pre–hangover

so you don't have to
punish yourselves
for joy

not that there's
much around me

it's all in the write

use of weapons

when i was youth
another kid said
he saw me
as captain kirk

fecking eedjit
but i tell you something
i still love the complement
it's totally wrong

i have no career
of a mythical hero
i've fenland meandered
I'm a nowhere man

anyway   ANYWAY
i've seen the rebooted trek
fucking idiot's still wrong
my ego's still glowing

the myth is a hoot
the comparison's bollocks
but i like the idea
of doing the plotting

to command my own chair

i'll make my own chair

make my own chair

damn you banks

With apologies to Iain M Banks.

big city blues

big city blues
i'm calling this
the big city blues

big city blues
big city?
the big city blues

a big city's london
a big city's bruxelles
power and capital ...

big city blues
i'm calling this
the big city blues

this place
the capital
of selected ancestors

this place
a capital
of aspiration

a big city
small
a big city

small city blues
i'll call this
the small city blues

smog coda

if i don't believe
i don't look

if i don't look
i don't find

if i don't look
i don't find
what i don't seek

if i don't find
what i don't seek
i don't find
what i don't believe

how many believers
accept
the gift
of what they don't believe

how many non–believers
look

the gods are buggers
i don't believe in them

i wish they'd return

the complement

la voiture don't care

les élégances
qui créeront *ich hoffe*
la révélation rose du monde

une révolution
du monde

j'elles voudrais *touch*
j'elles voudrais *caress*
j'elles voudrais *adore*

elles ne me verront jamais
je suis de quel univers
ce n'est pas cet

cettes
ont été le trou
de mon histoire

elles seront
die Geschichte
für meine alten Wünsche

where does
this resonance
originate

where does
this resonance
originate

it's always
always
been

the me kid
admiring
the beautiful

déesse
une rue avait
petites peurs

la voiture
don't care

was habe ich

a few nights ago
i found myself
writing
eight poems

tonight
i find myself
writing
ten

was habe ich

four years

it's interesting
the difference
four years

last time
the longest far
across a crook
te *belgië*

naar nu heeft
belgische
britse ierse
slechte hopen

and chance
in kerela
in Changchun

exercised

the have to visit
the fill the forms
the stamp the tick

thomas street
    vijf
water
    vier
apollo's wart
    vier en meer
offmoreland
    één
duck street
    twee
the gentlemen of tax
    twee

i'm grateful
honest
exercised

small barrier

me told me
a month
to start

start & stop
made the place

the barrier
start

once i've the seen
can grow

it's make the seen
the barrier

the logiciel semantic
create all the source
parfait

create
each phoneme
before use
reuse

much speaking
without speaking

box tick

from a pocket denting
you know
it would hardly fit

to a super computer slip
with box tick features
without box tick can use

where am i going

now we've mostly got
the record collection
that used to take a wall

and we've mostly got
the book collection

the photograph collection

i'd like to have
the texture
to touch collection

where are we going

now we've box tick features
with box tick can use
without box tick why

is there information
that won't be pocketed

are we going there

it's such a cliché
poets and sense
but where are they

sight
    strained
sound
    good
smell
    not even understood
touch
    no
taste
    nope
balance
    in the box
and the undocumented

so much for the singularity
so much for the soon

just a leak

i'll come back to these
but the older me
believes
they won't work

there's the deeper me distressed
at that

the deeper me's the writer
every time is right
i never ken

wij zullen zien

but i'll have to
refind
autres langues

en andere wegen
this is just an identity set

WRONG
think you silly arse
think what set this off
it's a leak

la fin

eight

acht

acht

huit

otto

eight

acht

acht

huit

otto

fin

(fat chance)

1983

imperialisma
sweet nights

my photos
depuis vingt cinq ans
me no know

those images
that place
the party
deux cent delight

my gut recalls

vingt cinq ans

it's idiotic
depuis vingt cinq ans

seeking faces
depuis vingt cinq ans

as if the faces
depuis vingt cinq ans

were the faces
sans vingt cinq ans

e la fotocamera

i too
new place
touristico
e la fotocamera

excited the here
catch
identi–sight

i critique
yet i screw shoot still

how can i a fresh
when every there
snap handed

need to know
the see unseen

need to luck
the full awe

need to empath
stranger mouths

or studied the before

werde ich nicht zu frozen

like reels

the tailoring

imperialisma
the smoke
the history

wind glist flags
identity
but flags attend
to exclude

mass autocages
tourist
breeze

a nation's
no cult
no way

but i wish
they'd not adopt
the tailoring

routemaster

i do actually love this city
its thousand styles of chutzpah
the rich of different

it's an orchestra
the conductor's
the bus

you don't have to travel
the vision

to have
the vision

the house

their bouncers
submachine guns

their career
i refused

they were bounced
liberty to

high stream

high stream
press gut
joy resign

light song through
sigh promotion
gender rasp

but i distant
a starlight
lose manity

animal fall
songstream soiled
broke turing

skinside experience
all no trade
no struggle

yet twinside as
sidehigh railway
downside

normally false

when sounds
say extreme
normally false

but sounds
say extreme
known true

you do
Was

stone rush

stone rush leave
out glass crib glance
private eclectic archordia
imagined immense

no vitesse
tiny place
delay huge
green tarmac

imagined immense
no vitesse

distant band

distant band
wood dawn
ground mist lit
trees risen
cloud

night disconnected
alienation inner
two skin tradition
me for three
no

dive undived
dawn pittance
camera the coldest air
i still
scarred

think not
too late for warmth
think
cold ash fire

cold ash

as sid said

writ application
then extra
being first *zelfstandig*
"can you confidence the girls"

i'd have writ
"no clue"
the mother intercepted
"no problem"

i wish
i'd sneaked the night
ripped the envelope

stole the lie
stung inside
spat my true reply

as sid said
"regrets
i have a few"

a warning shade

the minister of stuffed
"a warning shade
in outside sight
antithesises
intensity"

which rather buggered this

an absence of wanting the here
that's the warning shade
accompanied duty

like i'm the maiden aunt
i am the maiden aunt

just a slice

the hide tide
fails to stem the streets
just a slice

president shan't's gift
that denier's *Gift*
wird

air a water bright

air a water bright
black speck summer bite
bike along green wheat

stop each we grab a hedge
lift lift lift the field
what's beneath our glory

shake unshaven off
and fold fold
what's beneath the glory

it takes a day
to fold fold
what's beneath our glory

and underneath
underneath
you're beneath our glory

technology of choice

"choice

earn a ton
most people earn a half

earn five
most people earn a grand

surprisingly
most select
the first"

why the surprise
mister economist

absolute's for religion
remote–destructing conscience

money's for society
relative share

no not belief

the act
had me withdrew

over
people wound joy loud

later
an unrelaxed chat

another praised like sun
the act snatched sharply on

just because it doesn't work for me
doesn't mean it doesn't work
it merely means it doesn't work for me

confidence
no
not confidence

belief

no
not belief

being

our rounded city

our rounded city
where
down the deepest haze
sea

our only city
where
down distortion haze
seething

our prison city
where
down the wall–less gaze
horizon

honourable mrs council official

no
honourable mrs council official

i'm not alone through
(example of pain relief mechanism)
choice

i'm alone through
(example of pain relief mechanism)
steep mountains

(example of pain relief mechanism)
here's a flaw
writing half asleep

once the computer's on
the poem's
(example of pain relief mechanism)
vanished
oi
who said something about
the universe's self–editing mechanism
at work

oh
me

drunk

in england
ephemera's vandals

in ireland
good time gargoyles

chum like

chum like
introducing mountain hills

in catastrophe slopes
i saw grass reflecting

15 year glass
25 year glass

failure grass
that's now reflected

himbeeren

track
für Fotos

wildflowers
blackberries *himbeeren*

homes so abandoned
roofs have fruited

cat gut

met mijn fotografie
what's missing
is the model

the image
comment tension

the cat gut

cast

meanwhile
played on the pod
the musician's on holiday

it's not like he's nothing to say
it's more the way to say
the photographer was quicker

the poet's
still king
of the kitchen

the lover
would like to be born
please

objectivity's a myth

whose eye finds the image
who angles the horizon
who saturates the colours

who exposes the light
who starks the unique
who marks the best

the guy with the eye
the camera
the conscious aware

objectivity's a myth

or can the objectors
blind to non–human waves
capture the harmonics unknown

does the objective eye
with his triangle degree
photo just squares in the norm

his attempt
to reflect
the collective subjective

objektivity's a myth

no refreshment

all the wondrous art
is sod all
unconnected

no value
with no push
no pop

wondrous was sarcastic
ok

promotion
as civilisation's
jolly good hot cup of tea

no promotion
no connection
no refreshing

i'm better
at bullshit
in French

coda

the lover
would like to be born
please

darkening

darkening grows
carnivore plant
pulls to you

darkening day
wisting sun
slowth

> *events*
> *deign me write*
> *season's being–be*

darkening's brace
ice rain
absent

there is no cold
where's the rain
where's the pull

image hunt

interruption

i the image hunt
found
not the hunted

the glass
a painting
the drinker
white shapes
chase

behind me
telewele nod
pseudo–pindar

i done the image hunt today
not the shapes i sought
caught

köln

overture
nach berlin
von brüssel
ICE
köln

nach berlin
von schiphol
ICE
köln

fugue 1
one track
a metre apart
ahead behind

one end
a metre apart
ahead behind

fugue 2
i'm not on this track
you're not on this track

you're not on this track

i'm not on this track

fugue 3

i'm far far ahead

just look at me here

you're far far behind

just look at you here

fugue 4

a metre apart

ahead behind

a metre apart

ahead behind

incident

incident–

—ally

incident

the time

in skirts

policemen dance

incidentally

a Gilliam

incident

show

—ally

incident–

incidentally

   this road

      has a cliff

this road

   don't skirt

      said cliff

this road
   old road
      new cliff

incidentally so
still a show
it is

is it
   a show
      a cliff

they're your wheels
   the cliff
      they're

dancing skirts

pinocchio's nose

the beer glass   horizontal
as though the guy's
grown pinocchio's nose
thick

the drinking up
ship in a bottle

forget this
he likes the beer
in shattered colour
paranoid texture

relaxed
a working man's cut
and cap

a sky of rags
no storm
just bloody disturbed

the guy's relaxed

i don't get the oily footprints
running up the neck
blot on the temple

what kind of mechanic
does that

two old

the moment is cheers
two older pals
drinking men's caps
olive green jackets
brown pullovers

in yorkshire
they'd be landrovers

the background's a cold wall
slaking rain for itself

coda coda

and a barstool corner guy
bluetooth ear

milk monitor badge
flashing siren blue

his middle–age
child mascara

shiva mary's son

dublin coast watch
thousand metre
irish sea over
roman firework pulse

suppression celebration
fawkesian terror held
old *di* victor
christian insurrection

blazen rockets rise
prime fight flight
seemingly we over
tease our fail

they've ever thought
stutter sparks glim
stone army to me
might night wait

our retry our retry
this year every year
retake *lloegr*
for shiva mary's son

above

above
straight bowed wood slots left right
light brown pine
texture growth
slots a shadow back

pine table legs fan pine top
grain summarised scrolls
pine arms aside clot zebra
pine floor wide   charcoal marble
two board square hard dance floor

frieze fawn wall script enlarged
hindu arabic hebrew
my ignorance grasps

solid shine
reception vaguely odd
huge space lone youth
cupboard doors colours cloth
drawing room   elderly ladyflowers
forty years
seen on sets
since

number number

number number
junky chant
stop

beer taste is toothpaste

juke config
chant restart
has each human de–

toothpaste is beer taste

what a dull poem
bureaucracy disconnect
weeks
organise & lust

beer taste is toothpaste

lust
i forgot the how
a detest effect
this species' ware

toothpaste is beer taste

i left my cat

in san francisco

and then the cornflakes would not fight

i left their nest a frightful site

—wenty t—

—wenty five t—
—ost my heart i—
—will pow—

—ill pow—
—ll pow—
—l po—

—enty fi—
—gy in the win—
—and and and—

empty

beloved

old peoples' bars
in *belgië*
play the music
beloved
of their old peoples'
dead parents

&
the pre–metro
on

feel
graves above
warmth

more

―――――――

(more music
to be dead
to)

―――――――

conflicted

conflicted
A♯
sat not seated

plain
B♮
i'm not

D   E♭
that's yesterday's
beer

an empty
perfect fifth
C below

no mood
to walk
tho' balance
walked
two weeks ago

a girl a splash
an alex harvey album

With acknowledgement to the SAHB.

je vais la vie

who'd believe
butterfly stomping
hobbified

exaggerated graveyard
tullamore
première scene

seller
he sold me apple lore
en PC
*l'*insensitive resent

so fat
not quite meet
my arms

tension pleasured
T stretched
tunnel cleft
pet pet

can't breathe
fingers sliced
wire neck
back head butt

garotte
film fail

doze doze
non
je l'ai la vie
paris

that was this morning

you know you've got problems
when you flush the bog
& it doesn't refill

that was last night

of course dozy idiot here
used it this morning
then remembered

that was this morning

so i rang the landlord
woke the poor bugger up
he was round pretty quick

that was this morning too

turned out the guy downstairs
came in drunk and collapsed
didn't notice the cataract

that was last night

so the plumber came
cursing hard working
ripped out the floors

that was this morning

i just packed
the landlord saw and agreed
i'm in an hotel

that was this morning too

i reckon he'd skimped
an overflow's been overflowing a month
now his luck's overflowed

that was misjudgement

but now
i don't feel i've a home
i'm in a hotel with no bed to go back to

that's not nice

airport

black
lit eyes red
immobile

a triangle
drifts

crawling
fascination

black
lit eyes orange
pulse

a cylinder
flows

crawling
distraction

black
lit eyes blue
immobile

cones

power

crawling

wind

black

lit eyes white

voyage

reflectors

pwn

crawling

crawled

cracked

desolée

désolée
mais en notre pays
nous n'avons plus eu
des langues compréhensible

les bâtiments deviennent
la neige monte

avant vous venez ici
vous devez habiter ici

des arbres boudent
les voitures fument ses chauffeurs

le trottoir chante
les oiseaux jouent le foot

strangers' pavement

walking
strangers' pavement
voiciïng
foreign gaunt

tout les nouveaux
rongent m'entente
concordance

i feel l'*échec*
physique

im allen Spiegeln

promenade

today's new promenade
low below *le grand arche*
magnificent modernist high
purity the hearty hail

lines sheer the up across
counting class countless glass
perceiving cells their rhythm
walk ambitious met

rare fresh my differ eyes
thousand here thousand see
côte à côte a thousand worn
strong camera eyes my fresh

slippery light icy night
high ground slide around
the skim edge the knife low wind
ça n'est pas romans c'est ça

musique sans musique

swing sing the nearer beat
diva crescendo high
hush harmony brush
tune between to go

in a conversation regular
new attention's sweet

train tracking rabid
lyric acid flute
make synth mange
off music

given presence
i'm invert

you know the rhythm
you know the tune
you know the style you get
set

sherbet

sherbet

sherbert

shearbert

shear flirt

sher flirt

her flirt

ha!

headache

i wouldn't mind so much
had this headache
earned itself

it's stolen the day
an irritation colleague
a breeding–eyed misfortuned

i'll be here tomorrow
i'll have had my sleep
it won't

contrails

a land
  of bright
    sky swings

the ropes may be contrails
  nothing more
    that frozen adventures

falling out the back of
  disappointed
    holidaymakers

but the seats are
  hard and solid
    dedicated myth

the kind
  that kill
    by inattention

i walk across them everyday
  ice on a black bridge
    three stories up

café noir français

i'm over the metro
there's no northern rumble
just tasty orange and coffee
dark space delight

weakly hotel hopping
afford & chaseable cheap
desalubrious archaic
arrondissament's borough yeah

bienvenue identikit architecture
that's the storey count
that's the window style the guests to fail
that's the fence of iron low

that's the form dictated
ok you can stop transcribing now miss jones
you ceased to exist
ten centuries ago

when jesus walked on ice
and again a while back
when dictaphone went bust
that's the specie progress

the pseudo lives

child me dreamt
solo ships so human
centuries between
depart arrive
pesudo lives spent
virtuality

then's tomorrow
projected onto death
my hymnen my alien
my familiar cosmology
an uneared cat
projected onto death

all that presume
our height our senses
our physiology our most everything
as though every ten billion years
resulted in another us
a so ordinary us
stuckist evolution
yeah that's the evidence alright

property

i should be allowed
to drive dangerously
if i desire
it's my car

i should be allowed
to shoot to you
if i desire
it's my gun

i should be allowed
to nonvaccinate
if i desire
it's my child

i should be allowed
to occupy
if i desire
it's my army

i should be allowed
to noneducate
if i desire
it's my child

monochrome and wasp

rings monochrome & wasp rig
leggings rise the soft *cent metres*

cent metres
some *mals du nuit* are daft

i presume the snakes
were a consequence
of a biological business meeting
interrupted
before memory rebegan

walking me not me
yellow green
eyeless street curb
small edge gravity
daily curb

it was the powerlessness

this city
je ne sais quoi

the leggings
a perfectly normal young lady
a metre off

an automatic descent

an automatic descent
escalator aging
rotating rubbing

grandfather
complaining
small me ran into

the sister
an automatic up
a slightly shorter beat

into metro
i descended down
clapping music

With acknowledgement of Steve Reich's "Clapping Music".

le soleil libre

nous pouvons construire

un réunion plus de faire

si le fox du foxtrot danse mauvais

si la grande arche est tombé

si je ne comprends pas exactement que tu ne dis pas

si tu ne comprends pas exactement que je ne dis pas

wij kunnen maken

een dan bereide afspraak

als de fox van de foxtrot danst slecht

als de koning hebt in de straat geslapen

als ik begrijp niet precies

wat je hebt niet gezegd

als je begrijpt niet precies

wat ik heb niet gezegd

nee

vergeet de maken

denkt een morgen vrij

ontbijten met dageraade licht

wij praten alles

onder een vrije zon

non

oubliez des construits

pensez un matin relâché

un café et un croissant

nous parlons tout

sous un soleil libre

a trawler

c'est difficile d'écrire
quand écrire n'est pas acceptable

het is moelijk scrijven
waneer scrijven is niet welkom

j'ai connu ta face publique
un fôret
tu as presenté vos arbres
beaucoups et grands
en cendres

there was a grand open sea
a trawler at night sought
so long sought
but when the catch was caught perhaps
"what have we done"

natuurlijk
ik heb de fôret pas vert gevraagt
la gardienne stood shocked
hebt een anworted gegeven
maar haar trawler storm *en niet*
wat heb ik gekennen doen

und liebden

als du bist ein wolf
alles friedlich sind die lagen
du laufst mit wölfe
zu alles grünen alles grossen
alles bergen alles frei
liebden

mais tu habites
du monde des hommes
uw natuur hoort niet
uw natuur hoort niet

gaten

come through the gate
how dare you come near the gate
please come through
oh my god i've let you through the
gate go back go back

come through the gate
how dare you come near the gate
come in i'll lock you in
come in i'll lock you out

ik zet
ik waat
ik wil praten
in dit land van gaten
ik ben niet een gaten gebruiker
morgen
ik wil gaan
ik vind thuis

news story with translation

il y a un mois
a long time ago far far away
que le parti poétique
an evil empire extended
avait elu au maire
across the world

aprés ce événement surpris
in a poor house
le nouveau marie
in a forgotten town
monsieur blaireau
a destiny child
a annoncé sa programme
was born
aesthetique catholique pour les toutes

la nouvelle politique
he grew to have
a une grande thème
great inspiration
que toutes les actions d'etat
he made a way
doivent être poétique
to rêve freedom

rêve

rêve

French pour revision

rêve

& the leakage

rêve

your psyché your scala

rêve

bloating upwards

rêve

scarlatti translated twice again

rêve

dark opera house sans audience

rêve

tenor in green

rêve

rising up floating

rêve

singing the black door song

rêve

he stings

rêve

pops

rêve

fades

rêve

the stage is empty unstained

rêve

the night is water

break

break
this is like it was
you know break
rush outta forced columns
like er out
to hard blue dark
play & racket make
knee cut asphalt
social like
playground pocket horrific
learn to unfear
constrained fifteen minute incidental
not be
talking not disbelieving
a wanker
a critical alienation

sargasso

mais avec les heures
nous avons créé
nos petits sargassos
un moment

je ferai
permettez moi
à jouir
de l'espoir

stamping

see a face
lincoln at arafat
lead a performance
stamp

party
entrance fee
paid for the bar
no staff

black table
white spot
spilt cloud

actually
that guy's
poncing

clatter

bark once for yes
none for no
what's clatter

marshally
exclude group coalesce
unhello *les toutes*

social skills very
"ooh look difference
let's hog ourselves"

bore like a mining machine

hier

soon
i will stop using
email

in future
please contact
my wife

... si vous avez acheté le billet il y a deux semaines quand il y était moins cher ...

his prognosis collapsed
please let their love its end days

j'avait décidé ne pas venir
il y a deux semaines

des mondes

un monde plat
la terre cature
craintes de nos ancêtres
nos rapports savant

je regard le grand *arse*
une femme indienne
son rituel de la danse
bollywood laugh crass

tealight through a water glass
raita reflected

olympus mons
extraordinary
nothing to that single light

we poison we all poison

>dammit
>i have the tense attack
>that precedes a

colonising the ripe
wild city food all food
they don't see us
they don't see us
rats in the metro
underneath sleepers
dark in the light wires
taking on machinery
we grow
we grow

and organise
yes organise
and when our time is right
we poison
we all poison

>dammit
>i have the tense attack
>that precedes a

colonising the ripe
wild flesh food all food
they don't feel us
they don't feel us
bugs in the bloodstream
under the aware
knives to the nerves
taking out machinery
we grow
we grow

and collect
yes we collect
and when our time is right
we poison
we all poison

    dammit
    i have the tense attack
    that precedes a

colonising the ripe
wild dogs food we food
they won't see us
they won't see us
ego in the argument
undermining reason

knives to the evidence

subverting sense machinery

we grow

we grow

and organise

yes organise

and when our time is right

we poison

we all poison

    dammit

    i have the tense attack

    that precedes a

the face

the face through *arrondissement* glass
the face in dialect
the face a century ago

no night breathes out
no night seen
no night lady wanders
no night
no

two girls their men distain
boxers cauliflower

faces
nights
trois

overtired
over

out

café matin

clatter spoon bright
make coffee dull
pack cup hollow
clash dish dumb

collect change shallow
turn page fries
speak word shadow
open door strain

walk *rue* rhythm
pull case wags

mild hurt

there's a mild hurt
where i cut my finger
nail

there's a mild hurt
where i cut my love
out

there's a mild hurt
where i cut my ciggy
need

there's a mild hurt
where i cut my sanity
in

for tidiness
as if i ever
caught that

come out into the cold sun

"so wonder if he looks down"
as if there's such an up

if reality's uncomfortable
is fantasy reasonable

if the end
is inevitable
why bother with the fear

welcome to the wonder world
your ten moments
in the hologram illusion

join the mature
come out into the cold sun
it's bright

it seems

it seems it was my fault
we didn't get together
well actually it wasn't
but i'm grateful we didn't

i don't like to hate
as much as i'd have hated

it seems it was my fault
we didn't unite
well actually it wasn't
but i'm grateful we staid

i don't like to hate
as much as i'd have hated

it seems it was my fault
we didn't glue
well actually it wasn't
but i'm grateful we fled

i don't like to hate
as much as i'd have hated

a large room

a large room
   for a small one
diminishing
chair
   side–table
     two–bed

bedcover red
   yellow pillow
grey
   by ancienting

industrial dust
   varnish floorboard
plain wall
   once cream blind

the neighbour's grey
   bushy moustache
unshaven
   silver morning
     at 6pm

gorgeously foreign

    local

were it not for the no cooker

    i'd live it

after the funeral

st. pancras
that greater arch
black locos
steaming
still

raincoated man
grey
vital
bounded up
"hello
how are you?"

grey light
day light

the uncle
from king's cross country

three minutes
ran out

hesitation
ran out

excuses

ran out

black

ran out

the swag

swansong
swag
shining green
descends descends
circles times
of other air

like all the times
i manipulate
to isolate
me

black tyres
black asphalt
black rough
slow roar

at lamarck
i'll climb
catch the sky
spark

my images
miss content
same content
circles

rattus frankenstein

self–propelled gloves
garden waste grasped
brown black grey–matt
temperamented sweet

i see these molly creatures
unaggressive unlike their english
i do not feel the wish
to drop kick

untouched

some say

untouched unedited

me

i rools me tules

she speeds past

legs stride a slow step
she speeds past
bike

lips sounds a slow speech
she speeds past
brain

legs strikes a slow strife
she speeds past
fate

lust struts a slow mad
she speeds past
dammit

the wind

the wind
it says
it wants to brush your dance
a cool cavort

but you see it
unconsciously
automatically
play with another

come

come
we'll have the railway laid
the town will be bright
the bunting will slant

came
trekked across the marsh
half–cut forest
bodies of songbirds

low

low broken grey
cart distant horse
green ivy body wheels
horse arch keel

techno cocoon buds
disc diesel scratch shake
again taking me away
toy waterbirds boy aside

techno cocoon phones
high dawdle race speed
tower *gare* tower *gare*
architecture i majesties go

green on green

there was an un among the trees
green on green   green all green
two met bracket glade
green on green   green all green
sun is shone on forever
as when i 'ere farsaw

sham rain sound   coldly down
"if you go that gap i'll cancel you
they've working class window glass"

common sounds

common play sound say
    we've yours
soon say foul say
    we've yours

tempted tormented
    we've yours
returned retempted
    we've yours

common play sound say
    we've yours
common stay play stay
    we've yours

hear these listen their
    we've yours
music mash night crash
    we've yours

listen their music
    laugh at you
listen their music
    laugh at you

so i adore so
so the real so
a never met so
lifelong oh

ugly

ugly
it seems a choice
for movement reduces

hillock bruises
estuary sweat
the cleavage
a consequence of nuclear waste

i could mention the conditions
that leave that face unchoiced

when songbirds are murdered
i find i presume intent

laugh

bombarding dead conversation
mock music laughs at you
slash your taste

sneering egotism dress police
style of blank imitation
slash your face

money money money money
money money money money
money money money money
money money money money

your fault
you chose the wrong parents

saint pancras

empty train alongside
occupied reflections
narrowing

second crowd
stand beyond strangeangled
awaiting a sunlit bus

the world that should be dull
is brighter   sometimes
i want to slide through

depressive face
reflecting smile
rain reflecting life

heading out

"one ..."

headmistress voice
difficult taming
contrapuntal child

fuck you for that
so that's how you think
gobsmacked
humanity

of course i've nothing to say
an invitation to love
is no childwhere

where the fuck are you coming from
why are you here
of course i zero

in my place you imply me
no you shall not
i am for beyond the moon

i ciao

"... is ..."

after shock

chair you're in
a wave   a one dimensional
bâtiment bateau   bigger bow

woman neighbour
cat   cat on alert
lorry low growl

terra infirma
too small to cause care
small is still scare

drunk no drink engineer no djinn

that comment ... about needing ... damn well playing ... you were just ... weren't ... l'histoire still plays ... i know i've ... sinds ... i know you've spoke i'm ... l'europe ... i don't want ... again ... i hate making ... i hated ... it's easier middle class to ... but ... it right after i'd ... my will ... her dose of non accidental ... that was no ... middle class i shouldn't ... a secret weapon ... pure blue ... italian title ... a tenner in error genuinely in error ... my italian aristocratic heritage speak speak ... the bottom of the ... it's still the ... out of that idioicy asap ... misled by a mad re-publican ... asked spot the structure ... that's a slapped ... can be bigger than the piece ... still the slapped ... for a while ... spotlit hint of bigger steel ... rhythm doesn't have to be repeated to be rhythm ... come for a weekend break he said ... i say ...

five

five
    understand his song
years
    can only sing
old

skeletal march

apparently

1920s

giant men

skeletal march

betcha now

concrete seas

flying fish

tube metal

dramming

why the dull

excitement

mild cold

wow

the rasp

rasp
heart
buzz
depress
clash

i fool
but
met
atmosphere
ever fail

i know x3
caution crap
atmosphere
ever wrong

hint
converse
desire
no be

rasp

wrong city

wrong country

wrong distance

but

rasp

bloody useless

i am

rasp

i detest

weapon

birthright

rasp is

out

out
now
fox in the chicken hole
out now

madame
je travaille
ou est mon dejeuner

enough days
for the small chance

discard the loudmouths
the liars those press
who enfear you

calculate
discard the numb–ers
real the numbers

so there i was
doing the straight work
& a *functionnaire* fuck–up

insurers fear

so sorry

go

go now

go

madame

s'il vous plait

mon ordre

one in a million

likely to happen

seconds in a month

what

you've not asked

why don't you wonder

shortsighted

shortsighted
that's me

mild distance
feels fake

those rare times
i glass focus
to closer

i look down
closer
terre exact
closer
feet they walk
closer
nothing drags
closer
it's all so
closer

i must be shorter
glasses
they shrink you

foul guilt

in these times
i don't feel easy
photographing stranger kids
their child selves
making smile

that three year old
gorgeous blue white summer dress
striding small
in the sun's
simple grin

perfect image

parijs

pollution stained ceiling
smoke faded office
an engine on his back
assisted runner
very clean
mind faces you
points
      out

behind
not quite contrasted out
an engineer
feeds her unicorn
josephine   **&**

        in black electric blue
         an agent
        lightning abounds
        anger
        see his angerscars
        nothing shy
        blusher than angerpack
        a rage flower
        has turned
            laps

&

relaxation café
belgian beer irish sun
wish you were here
ho ho

&

actor expressive face apoplexy embarrassed instruction
actrice bodypaint expressive stance feeding   feeding

college kid

when i's a college kid
a reputation nerd
a then my age girl
a stranger
"you wouldn't beat a woman
would you"

it took me a delay
"only
if she asked me
nicely"

her face responded
confuse
pity

i'd sought
blush

cold day

light slight pressure
cold day cold sway
remains of cold away
mon tête

light slight pressure
tired eyes wired eyes
remained night fried eyes
mon tête

light slight pressure
sore head bore head
deux heures dead head
mon tête

slight light pressure
night flight bright might
so hot my blood
my head

moment

writing in a reasonable breeze
about to meet a familiar beer